From The Heart of Africa

Short stories from Rwanda

Ti'

Multicom Printing & Publishing

5th Edition, 2021

Multicom Printing & Publishing
P.O. Box 3653 Kigali-Rwanda
E-mail: multicom@multicomplus.com
Website: www.multicomplus.com

First published in 2009

ISBN: 9966-05-169-4

Edited by Kristen Shane

Graphic Designs by Mucyo Espoir

Illustrated by Kofi Kankolongo

ACKNOWLEDGEMENTS

I would like to express my gratitude to Julien Kagabo, Chantal Veilleux, Janvier Ndolimana, Mariette Utamuvuna, Charles Rwabagina, Tony Muteti, Kristen Shane and Kofi Kankolongo for their support in the accomplishment of this work.

This book is dedicated to my Creator.

AUTHOR'S NOTE

This book of short stories is intended for both young and adult readers. Senior readers will find it valuable for Rwandan community's way of life while lower secondary and upper primary readers will also find it useful for grammar, vocabulary and reading comprehension.

It is a collection of imaginary stories from Rwanda that embrace the whole cultural structure of the Rwandan society. These stories were ingeniously invented by our fore fathers who used names of people, animals or places and set them against the forces of nature. The outcome of this teaching method was an effective tool for imparting norms and values to the youth. Although the stories seem to have taken place hundreds of years ago, they are still relevant to today's challenges worldwide.

Culture and literature are interdependent and remain the most reliable means of disseminating important virtues in a society, worldwide. In a reciprocal way, these shared virtues create a bond that unites a community and gives it a common hope and vision.

Key cultural virtues such as love, courage and patience, as well as tolerance and humility feature prominently in this book because they form the concept of a gentleman. It is this concept which determines a society's sustainability and guarantees its stability.

Like most societies worldwide, man in Rwanda has always dominated in all major activities. However, literature students will marvel at the unsurpassed level of forgiveness, courage and wisdom from both men and women as demonstrated in some stories.

The objective of this book is to revive the above mentioned virtues through Rwandan literature in the young generation as a catalyst for a meaningful development that is based on a common conscience

Read on!
Timothy Njoroge

TABLE OF CONTENTS

MUTINDI

There was once a rich man who lived happily in Umutara. The man owned a large herd of healthy cattle that dotted his swath of land. His land extended from Muvumba River to Rusumo Falls. The fertile land produced a variety of crops that were exported to neighbouring Karagwe, Burundi and Bugesera. He married a beautiful young woman and soon after, the couple had a baby boy who added flavour to their already enjoyable life. They called him Mutindi. However, the wife could not give birth thereafter and this brought some frustration to the couple. The man's friends started mocking him, claiming that he was not useful to the country since his household could not provide enough men to defend the nation in case of invasion. So they advised him to marry another wife, which he did.

The second wife gave birth to many boys and soon, all his attention turned towards her. The man had no time for his first wife and her only son. One day, his first wife told him:
"I know that our nation needs many young men to protect it. This is as true as I am your wife while Mutindi remains your son."
"Listen, woman: you have failed me. A real wife must be a mother of many boys!" replied her husband.

From that time onwards, she accepted her situation as a rejected wife but decided to stay, for the sake of her son. Her husband never paid her any visit.

Meanwhile, the mother with many boys was given anything she wanted while her sons underwent intensive military training in which they excelled. The man started enjoying a remarkable recognition from his colleagues for being an exemplary citizen while his first wife lived in total neglect. When Mutindi grew up, he went to work for his step-brothers who always mistreated him. They had accepted to employ him on condition that he would never tell anybody that he was actually their brother. Soon, their father grew very old and thought that it was time to give them their inheritances. He called all of them, including his first wife's son. When they had gathered, he allocated all his wealth to the second wife's sons. Then he turned to Mutindi, gave him his walking stick and said:
"Son of the neglected mother, this is your

inheritance."

All his step-brothers burst into laughter. This hurt Mutindi so much that he broke down and cried. His father pulled him aside, held him gently and told him:

"My son, your inheritance is in this stick and Bagendwa, the secret well. Before you get married, go with this stick to that secret well and claim your share."

Mutindi's brothers continued mistreating him. But the mistreatment did not hurt him as much as their mockery did, because sometimes they would even refer to his mother who was already subdued by her own miseries, back at the neglected home. On many occasions, they would make fun of him by asking him to milk his stick so that his mother could drink. Soon after, their father died. Mutindi ignored all the abuse and continued working. When he felt responsible enough to marry, he said goodbye to his mother who wished him good luck.

He headed for the secret well.

His journey started at the first cock crow. By noon, he could see the imposing Nyarupfubire Hill far behind him. By the evening, the same hill looked like an ant hill. He felt very tired. "Where is the secret well? How far is it from here? How long will it take me to get there?" These questions preoccupied his mind throughout the journey. Sometimes, he was surprised by the distance he had covered, whenever he looked back.

He thought that it was enough for that day. In those days, it was part of Rwandan culture to welcome strangers and offer them food and accommodation as well as any other assistance that such a visitor would require. All this would be done free of charge and every citizen had to fulfill this duty. This made Mutindi feel safe, despite the fact that it was getting dark. Mutindi looked back again. In the horizon, Lake Ihema looked like a tiny pond. He marveled at how such a big lake could become a pond. He asked himself what had become of the huge hippos that lived in it. He thought that they had become insects.

"Phew!" he exclaimed.

"They will no longer be able to damage my beans. Whenever the harvest time approaches, they come to feast on my crops, as if I only work for hippos," recalled Mutindi in disgust.

The nearest homestead belonged to an old woman who had no children. He went in and was welcomed. The old woman asked him the purpose of his journey, of which Mutindi explained to her satisfaction. She offered him some food and showed him where to sleep. In the morning, she gave him some packed food to eat on the way and wished him good luck. During his journey his brothers' cattle keepers teased him. Others offered him milk and asked where he was going. He could hear some of them saying that he was going to commit suicide at Rusumo Falls. The evening found him near the Chief's homestead. He entered. The chief instructed his subjects to offer him accommodation only.

The following morning, Mutindi started off early enough and passed through maize, bean and millet fields. It was harvest time. He marveled at how the crops had done well that season. He approached a group of young girls who were harvesting millet. He greeted them and asked them where and how far the Bagendwa well was. The girls directed him and he followed their instructions. Towards sunset, he noticed that the footpath he was following led to a thick forest. A woman nearby wondered what the man was going to do in that forest. She got worried because she knew that it was dangerous, especially at that unusual time. She asked him where he was going and what he was going to do. Mutindi explained everything and the woman let him enter the thick forest.

The forest was dark and dense. Occasionally, he could see a group of wild animals playing in front of him and blocking his way. He would wait patiently and once they had gone, he would continue. Then, all of a sudden, he heard a very deep voice calling him by his name. He was baffled. The voice called him again. He started trembling with fear. Then the voice told him:

"Do not worry, Mutindi. Just tell me where you are coming from and where you are going. I will help you." Then Mutindi explained everything to the voice.

"I see!" the voice replied.

"You are almost there. However, I would advise you to stay here till morning so that you may not have to walk in the forest during the night."

Mutindi obliged as the voice continued:

"There is a big snake which must drink water from this well. There is also a stone in the middle of that well. When you reach the well, go straight to the stone and sit on it. When the snake arrives, let it drink water and swim. It will then come to you and toss you up in the air and catch you. Do not be afraid. Once it has done that, you also hold it, toss it into the air and wait for its instructions. You must follow everything it will tell you."

The following morning, he reached the well at sunrise. He noticed the stone in the middle of the well. He sat on it. He was day-dreaming when a sizzling sound attracted his attention. He looked in the direction where the sound was coming from and saw a giant snake that dived into the well. It drank water, and then swam. Sometimes, it would keep part of its tail in the water and spin the rest of its body in the air. It would then repeat the same exercise with its head or tail in the water at regular intervals. The more the snake applied its acrobatic skills, the more Mutindi got scared. He was about to take off when the snake seized him with its tail and threw him 10 metres in the air. He came down head-fast but the snake held him and tossed him up again.

It was Mutindi's turn to toss the snake in the air. He grabbed it and hurled it above himself, caught it mid air and tossed it again before catching it and placing it gently on the very stone he had been sitting on. Then the snake looked at him and said:

"You are the luckiest and the richest man on this land from now onwards. You will be blessed with many children and property. Just pick up your stick and go back. As you go, many large herds of cattle and their herdsmen will follow you. They will all be yours. Remember to follow the same way that brought you here. Give a young cow to the girls whom you found harvesting millet and a young bull to the chief who gave you accommodation."

The snake paused and then asked:

"Do you remember the old woman who gave you accommodation on the first day?"

Mutindi nodded timidly before the snake continued:

"You will stay with her and treat her like your mother. Let your own mother live with the old woman. All your step-brothers will henceforth pledge allegiance to you and you will be their leader."

Mutindi picked up his stick and everything became as the snake had said. He followed all its instructions and all was well, till his last day of his life. However, the feeling of being underprivileged continued haunting him throughout his life, as the word Mutindi implies.

RUHINYUZA

There was once a man called Ruhinyuza who had ten children. He had inherited enough land on which he grew crops to sustain his family. In those days, it was a custom for a man to have as many children as possible. In fact, couples who could not have more than two children were despised by the society. As his wife continued giving birth, the family grew larger every year such that in the end, his harvest could no longer satisfy their needs. The more the children grew older, the more the family grew poorer. One evening, Ruhinyuza summoned all his children and told them:

"My children, we do not have enough to eat and I can not expand our piece of land. Besides, your mother and I are too old to work for other people. This situation leaves us no other alternative except stealing."

The whole family, after seriously considering any other available option, agreed unanimously to their father's suggestion. That decision made each family member into a licensed thief. As soon as the decision had been made, Ruhinyuza left the house.

Kamanzi's house was only one kilometre away. He reached its compound. He could hear his heartbeat. He thought that his chest would burst any time. He pressed it with his left hand while the other one held a spear. Cautiously, he approached the door. He waited a little bit and then pushed it open. He tiptoed in and found everyone asleep. Kamanzi's wife had given birth to a baby girl that evening. The little girl and her mother were lying on a traditional mat in the living room. It was almost midnight. Suddenly, he heard a voice from above saying:

"Welcome to the world, little girl. You will grow into a very beautiful girl and everybody will admire you before being killed by an elephant's tusk at a very young age."

Ruhinyuza knew that it was the voice of God and felt a strong urge to challenge it. He changed his mind and decided:

"Let me see whether God really tells the truth."

He carefully went where the mother and the baby were sleeping, pierced his spear where he thought the baby was and left the house in

a hurry without taking anything. The following morning, he visited Kamanzi's house expecting to find them mourning because he thought that he had killed their baby. He was surprised to find that everything was normal. He had actually missed the target. Meanwhile, Kamanzi welcomed his friend and was very glad to inform him that his wife had given birth to a baby girl. Ruhinyuza could see the happy mother cuddling her beautiful baby.
"This is incredible!" he thought.
Ruhinyuza was offered some wine. He pretended to enjoy his host's reception but he soon got bored and went back to his house. The voice he heard on the day he had gone to steal was still vivid in his mind. He felt embarrassed. The fact that nobody saw him trying to kill the child was his only consolation.

Meanwhile, his economic situation improved slowly but steadily as some of his children grew old enough to fend for themselves. He had also married off some of his daughters and had received many cows as dowry. He had become a very important person in that village. However, his mind was preoccupied by what he did to his good neighbour, although nobody knew anything about it. The secret grew heavier as days, months and years passed. The thought of sharing it with anybody else scared him stiff. This situation was worsened by the fact that the very girl he had wanted to kill grew up into a very beautiful woman. Furthermore, he had become very rich and many people in that village had started urging him to marry her. In those days, it was acceptable for an old man to marry a girl who would be his daughter's age. He thought that it would be a good idea if he married her as it would reduce his burden.

He finally decided to marry her. He asked his servant to prepare a very good wine which should be ready within one week. When the wine was ready, he asked his friends and relatives to escort him to Kamanzi's home to ask for his daughter's hand in marriage.

Ruhinyuza's delegation reached his future in-law's home before noon. They were warmly received and the ceremony started immediately. They drank, sang and danced. Kamanzi agreed to give his daughter to Ruhinyuza, a fact that attracted thunderous applause and ululations from the crowd. One month later, he came to pay the dowry and was allowed to take his wife. That marriage became the talk of the season in that area as both the bride and the bridegroom were the village's most popular individuals. The bride had been exemplary in all household tasks while the bridegroom was mostly known for having seen both heights of any economic situation.

As his invited guests were enjoying themselves on the wedding day, the voice he had heard when the girl was born was still fresh in his mind. He looked at his new wife and appreciated her beauty. He remembered the night he had wanted to stab her. He remembered the morning he went to Kamazi's house and found that the girl was well. He could feel the wine taste that Kamanzi had offered him. Then he started imagining how an elephant will one day pierce his beloved wife with one of its tusks. All this made him feel very sad.

"Will the elephant come all the way from the forest to this village just to kill my wife? Will my wife leave the village to find the elephant in the forest?" he asked himself.

He could not find any answer. Everyone could see that he looked sad but none dared to ask him. They preferred enjoying their wine.

When the ceremony was over, he called his servants and instructed them never to let his new wife leave the compound. In order to ensure that it would be done, he asked them never to leave her alone. He even allowed them to use force to prevent her from venturing out if they found it necessary. He thought that in case the elephant came, those men surrounding his wife would kill it before it did her any harm. Then, he reassured himself and went about his usual business. The servants followed their master's instructions to the letter and their work was not very difficult as the woman proved to be extremely obedient.

One day while the young wife was basking in the early morning sun with her body guards, a stressed antelope dashed out of the nearby bush like lightning. An army of angry hunting dogs were after it. It was a very short but spectacular moment. The excitement made the new wife move towards the fence to see the scene more clearly. She stepped on something sharp. She felt an itching pain but ignored it due to the excitement. None of her body guards noticed the incident because she considered it so insignificant that she did not even alert anybody about it.

However, the pain persisted. She scratched her foot at the place that had been pierced. The wound was not visible but still painful. She thought that the pain would soon disappear but by noon, her leg had started swelling. By the evening, the pain from the swollen leg had become unbearable. Her husband called for the best medicine men in the area but the leg continued swelling. By midnight, she was dead.

"Surely, God must be a liar," he asserted angrily.

No elephant had been seen in the area for several years. Furthermore, her bodyguards had assured him that she had never left the compound since she got married and Ruhinyuza had trusted them.

In the morning, the husband went to inspect the place where she had been sitting the previous day. He instructed his servants to dig up the whole compound. Much debris was unearthed.

A protruding object near the fence attracted his attention. On looking at it closely, he was shocked to find that it was indeed a broken piece of an elephant tusk which had been buried there several years earlier. Suddenly, he remembered the elephant that had been killed there by hunters when he was still a young boy. He could not do anything to the bodyguards because they had followed his instructions and kept his wife within the compound. He then remembered the fateful night when he attempted to steal. He remembered the voice. He remembered the warm welcome that Kamanzi gave him the following morning. He started making arrangements for the burial. Many people came to mourn the young wife. They stayed at Ruhinyuza's home for a week.

Ruhinyuza kept quiet throughout the mourning period. Then he prepared some wine and invited all his friends including Kamanzi's family. When they came, he narrated how he had come to Kamanzi's house to steal and how he changed his mind when he heard the voice. He told them how he wanted to challenge God by killing the baby. He explained why he decided to marry her and keep her indoors so that no elephant would ever see her, only for her to step on a fragment of a decomposed elephant tusk that had been buried right where she was being heavily guarded.

He asked them to forgive him, adding that above all, he had learnt that God is really the Almighty.

The crowd forgave him for everything he had done. Everyone went home more convinced than ever that God means what He says.

THE ADVENTURES OF SEBAHIGI, THE HUNTER

There once lived a poor hunter along Akanyaru River, in the Southern part of Rwanda. He was unlucky with his traps.

He always found that they had caught inedible animals such as big frogs, snakes and rats. Sometimes, small predators such as wild dogs fell into his traps. His wife mocked him for failing to bring home any game meat like other hunters. All this made him feel very unfortunate. He resolved to keep rabbits as his source of meat. He then decided to move all his traps near the river because that was where all the animals went to drink water. The traps did not catch any animal there either. The situation remained the same for several months.

One day, as he was roaming the forest, he found that one of his traps had caught a lion. He was so angry that he lifted his spear, ready to kill it, when the lion told him:
"Sebahigi, do not kill me."
"Why should I spare you?" asked Sebahigi, and added:
"Do you spare us?"
"Have I ever eaten any member of your family?" asked the lion.

"I must kill you because you have eaten many of my friends. You are the enemy of mankind."
The lion said:
"Sebahigi, I know that you are a very poor man. I have watched you hunt in this forest for several years. I have come purposely into your trap so that I may save you from that uncomfortable situation. If you want to become the richest man on this land, then set me free. The choice is yours."

Sebahigi hesitated. He recalled how miserable he had been. He remembered his wife's mockeries. But then, he also remembered that the lion could eat him if he sets it free. He lifted his spear, ready to kill it. The lion asked him to think again in order to make a good decision. So he asked the lion:
"Are you sure that you will not eat me once I set you free?"
"Listen, Mr Sebahigi: We animals do not behave like human beings. Lions kill only when they are hungry. We never attack other

animals aimlessly. We even choose which animal to kill before we decide to attack. We are never jealous like you. Instead, we feel very proud when people prosper. Above all, we must prove our generosity. It is really up to you to choose," replied the lion.

Sebahigi thought again. He recalled that he was, after all, leading such a miserable life that if the lion ate him, his miseries would end there. On the other hand, the lion would perhaps keep its promise such that he actually had nothing to lose, either way. He decided to untie the lion.

The lion congratulated Sebahigi for his choice and told him:

"Follow me."

Together, they disappeared in the thick forest and soon after, they arrived in the land of lions where he was treated to a very warm welcome. There, every type of crop flourished: bananas, maize, beans and potatoes were plenty. However, the only food that was eaten in that land was meat. Any other crop was regarded as a flower.

Every hour or so, a dead antelope or buffalo could be brought to the king lion. Sebahigi got the opportunity to eat all the meat that he had missed for a long time. Though lions enjoyed raw meat, Sebahigi was free to cook the meat. Everyday was a holiday in that land. Soon, he got fed up with meat. He asked his host to let him go back to his village. The kind lion obliged and gave him a magic stick and told him:

"This magic stick is a special gift for your kindness. Once you reach home, find a safe place in the house and keep it there before you do anything else. Then come out of the house immediately. You will be able to understand the language of animals."

They said good bye to each other and Sebahigi left hurriedly. Being a hunter, he thought he had an advantage over other hunters because he would understand everything that any animal said. On reaching home, he did exactly as he was instructed and immediately found himself surrounded by loyal servants, in a palace-like home. His tattered clothes turned into beautiful robes that were only worn by kings. When he looked beyond the compound, he saw large herds of cattle, all belonging to him. He was indeed the richest man in the land. He marveled and wondered what could have happened if he had killed the lion.

As he sat down, his dog came, jumping happily around him as it wagged its tail. He patted it gently in return and whispered to it:
"You are now a rich man's dog."
One could easily tell that they had really missed each other. Then, another dog came and Sebahigi's dog went to greet him. It was a stray dog that paid frequent visits to Sebahigi's homestead. Both dogs had become intimate friends over the years. They sat down near him and started chatting.
"Hey! Did you know that there is going to be a very long famine in two months time?" asked the stray dog.
"Of course I know. I am looking forward to

eating a lot of meat. Just imagine! We are going to be very fat!" replied the other dog.

The dogs observed how fat the cows were and started salivating.
"If I were you, I would advise my master to accumulate a big stock of provisions for sale during the long famine," said the stray dog.
"Oh! Come on! It is unfair to take advantage of other people's misfortunes," said the other dog.
"But that is their nature! Human beings succeed by taking advantage of their friends' misfortunes," replied the stray dog.
"Oh, no! Then human beings must be the worst creatures on earth! In any case, my master would not understand our language. So it is even useless to try telling him." Sebahigi's dog said.

Sebahigi had keenly followed the dogs' conversation. He soon piled a large stock of provisions and before long, a severe drought occurred. All the crops dried up and nothing grew for two years. As a result, there was nothing to eat and many people as well as animals died of hunger. The only source of food was Sebahigi's stock which he sold at an exorbitant price to his emaciated neighbours. He grew even richer than he had ever been before. Finally, heavy clouds appeared in the sky and it started raining again. Plants reappeared and the land became green once more. Soon after, people started harvesting and life came back to normal.

After some time, the stray dog came to Sebahigi's compound to greet its friend.
"Did you notice how your master took advantage of his neighbours' misfortunes during the famine?" asked the stray dog.
"Yap," answered the other dog.
"My friend,"said the stray dog, "I am sorry to inform you that in two months, all the girls in this village will die of a plague. Only those who live on the other side of the river will be saved."

Sebahigi had again followed each detail of the dogs' conversation and on that very day, he went to the other side of the river to start building a new house and moved in immediately it was complete. No sooner had he moved to the other side of the river than all the girls in Sebahigi's former village died of a strange deadly disease. He came back to settle in that village long after the plague was over. All his eight daughters survived and he became the only father-in-law to all the young men in the village, which made him the community's most important man.

One fine morning, the stray dog came again. Both dogs started chatting under the tree where Sebahigi was seated. They observed that Sebahigi had escaped all the calamities and suspected that he had understood all their conversations. Then Sebahigi's dog said:
"Okay, that is good for my master, but the only problem is that he keeps all the information to himself. Why doesn't he advise his neighbours?"

The stray dog answered:
"Didn't I tell you that it is human nature to take advantage of their fellow human beings' misfortunes? I can assure you that we are lucky to be dogs. Anyway, I am sorry to inform you again that your master will die today."
"What!" yelled the other dog.
"Yes. Your master will die today at sunset."
"What should I do?" asked the other dog.
"Nothing. Absolutely nothing! You will simply watch your master die. However, he may survive if he returns the magic stick to the land of lions and loses all his wealth."

Sebahigi looked to the sky. He observed that it was still early. He knew he was going to die that day. He looked at all his wealth: his diamond, gold and other precious metals. He looked at his innocent wife and children. He had never taken time to appreciate how his own children were really special, for, he had spent most of his time trying to make himself rich.

He looked to the sky again. It was mid day. He observed his gardens. Flowers were blossoming. Birds sang happily in the trees. They flew from one tree to the other as if it was a holiday for them. He saw how happy they were and started feeling jealous of them. He started throwing stones at them. Whatever sound they made, he started feeling that they were mocking him. He could neither eat nor drink. He looked at the stick. He recalled how miserable he had been before receiving it. He seriously started choosing between death and poverty. Meanwhile, time pressed on…

In his situation, what would you have chosen?

MUGABO THE MIGHTY

Once upon a time, there lived a widower in Central Rwanda. He had refused to remarry for fear that a step-mother would mistreat his children. His friends and relatives had abandoned him, saying that they could not trust a man who did not have a wife. But the man stuck to his conviction until all his children became mature and self-reliant. One day, he brought his children together and told them:

"Your mother died when you were still young, but I decided to stay a widower because I feared that a step-mother would mistreat you. Now that you are big enough to fend for yourselves, I want to know what you would like to do for me in return."

Each, except the last born, said what he would do for his beloved father. When the last born was asked to say something, he kept quiet because he did not know what to say.

After a few months, the old man called his sons again. He slaughtered a fat bull and carefully roasted its meat for that particular occasion. He hoped that his last born would then say what he would do for him, but still the young man did not have anything to say. So, his brothers got very angry with him, started beating him and even chased him out of that family. As he was allowed to take with him whatever he wanted, he collected some pieces of roasted meat, packed them well and left. Whenever he got hungry, he would exchange some meat for other food and life went on until the meat was finished. He tried to persevere but his patience ran out after three days without eating. He finally decided to look for employment.

He asked a certain man to employ him. The man asked him:
"What is your name and what are you able to do?"
"I am called Mugabo the Mighty. The only job that I can do for you is to carry your tobacco pipe, Sir," said the young man.
The man told him that he could not employ somebody just to carry his pipe. He advised him to try his luck elsewhere.

Later that day, he met another man to whom he told the same thing and the man offered him a job. The young man was happy. For some months, the boy ate and slept well. Then one day his employer asked him:

"What did you say your name was?"

"Mugabo the Mighty, Sir."

"Are you sure you are Mighty?" asked the employer.

"Oh, yes! No man in this entire region can match me," answered the young man.

"Does that include me and the king?" asked the employer.

"Absolutely! I am mightier than both of you."

"Then I must go and report this to the king," threatened the employer.

"Go right ahead, Sir," replied the young man.

When they reached the king's palace, the employer said what the boy had told him. The king asked the boy whether that was true and the boy confirmed that it was true. Then the king said:

"Remain here so that I may confirm whether you are really mightier than any of us in this region."

One fine morning, the king asked the young man to clear a well that was infested by dangerous snakes and surrounded by a thick forest. That forest was inhabited by fierce animals such as lions, leopards and buffalos. The young man went there fearlessly and cleared the forest and the well. He killed any animal that approached him. After one week of hard work, he sent a message to the king to come and inspect the well. He added that if he wished, he could even bring his cows to drink water from it.

The king told his herdsmen to take cows to the well. When the cows had drunk water, the boy escorted them back to the king's palace. The herdsmen reported how beautiful the well was and the king was happy. But he was not fully contented. So, he thought of a more difficult task, just to test him. The king asked the young man to follow his men and carry out any orders that would be given to him.

Together, they walked until they reached a hard rock. They asked the young man to get firewood from that rock. They gave him an axe and told him that it should remain unscratched after the exercise. They left him there and went back to the king's palace. After they had left, the rock was struck by lightning. Immediately, a snake emerged and tied together the broken pieces of rock. The lightning struck again and placed the load on the young man's head. Then, a supernatural wind blew him and dropped him in the king's palace. Those who had given him that task arrived several hours later. They were all exhausted and too tired to talk. The king was amazed, especially when he observed that Mugabo looked fresh while the axe was unscathed.

A few months later, the king called for him again and gave him another test. He told him that there was a field, far away, that needed planting. He added:

"The field is already cleared. I just want you to

sow the whole of it with finger millet."
He gave him servants to help him carry the finger millet for sowing. But the field had not been cleared. In fact, it was a virgin bush. The servants left him there and returned to the palace. While he was still wondering how to approach the problem, a multitude of rodents in various species appeared and told him:
"Do not worry. We have come to help you."
As soon as they had finished saying that, they started burrowing the field and before the sunset, the whole field was ready for planting. Mugabo sowed his seeds and went back to the palace. After three weeks, the king went to inspect that field and was amazed. But the thought that the young man could clear such a large area of land within hours worried him. He wondered how all that millet would be harvested but he said to himself:
"He will be the one to harvest it, anyway."

When the harvest time approached, Mugabo asked the king for one hundred large baskets to keep the millet. The baskets were

made and given to Mugabo and one hundred men to carry them. The king instructed the servants to only carry them to the field and then come back to the palace as Mugabo alone would do the harvesting. The servants did as they were instructed. On the harvest day, birds of all species came, picked the millet and filled all the hundred baskets. They ate the rest as their reward. Mugabo sent word to the palace for people to come and carry the millet. When the king saw all this, he got even more worried and told Mugabo:
"I have confirmed that you are really a mighty young man. Now, I will send you to bring back my royal drums that were confiscated by another kingdom."
This time, the young man got scared. He even bade farewell to all his friends and colleagues because he thought he would never come back alive. He started feeling that he was very unfortunate to have been named Mugabo the Mighty. He knew that the king wanted him to do the impossible. He recalled that the foreign king had always defeated his

own king. All the same, he followed his king's instructions.

The journey was very long. After spending several days traveling, he met an old woman and asked her if she would let him stay at her place for one night. The old woman asked the purpose of the young man's journey. He explained to her everything. In the morning, the old woman told him:
"Go well, my son! On your way, you will see a homestead that houses two girls. One of the girls has a mark on the cheek. That is where you will have to spend your night."
Mugabo thanked the old lady and left in a hurry. Towards sunset, he noticed a homestead and saw two beautiful girls. One of them had a mark on the cheek. Then he remembered what the old woman had told him. He approached them and sought accommodation. When he was ready to leave that homestead, he heard a voice telling him:
"Hold the girl with a mark on the cheek and make sure that she does not escape you."

Immediately, lightning struck a huge tree that was in the compound. On seeing this, Mugabo's hosts asked him and the girl to leave their homestead right away. They told him to marry the girl if he wanted. Mugabo left the homestead with the girl. It soon became dark and they were forced to seek accommodation in another homestead. They were allowed to stay there overnight. In the morning as they were thanking their hosts for having been very kind to them, the girl smiled and lightning struck again. Their hosts got terrified. They asked the couple to pick whatever they wanted from the homestead but leave immediately. Mugabo and the girl decided to pick two spears. They left the place and continued their journey.

In the evening, they reached the kingdom's palace where the confiscated drums were kept. They asked for accommodation and they were allowed to stay there for as long as they wished. Mugabo spent most of his time spying. He wanted to know exactly where the drums were kept. It did not take him long to locate them. He then planned how he would get them out of the palace. He thought the best time to leave the palace was in the middle of the night when everyone was fast asleep. He told the girl to leave first and promised to find her ahead.

At around midnight, Mugabo tiptoed to pick up the two drums and left the palace immediately. He soon caught up with the girl and together, they ran as fast as their legs could carry them. They kept running till morning. By the time people knew what had happened in the palace, Mugabo and the girl were beyond reach. The king's guards did not even know which direction that Mugabo had taken. They gave up chasing the couple and forgot about the drums. When the couple reached the palace, the king was so delighted that he decided to appoint Mugabo the kingdom's prime minister. Soon, they invaded the kingdom that had confiscated the drums and defeated it. Mugabo served the king very diligently such that the kingdom prospered and grew more and more powerful.

NDUMUHIGI

Once upon a time, there was a couple that lived in Central Rwanda. They only had a son called Ndumuhigi. In those days, it was customary for any adult young man to spend at least two years working at the king's palace where he would learn various styles of martial arts, hunting, and good manners as well as Rwandan customs. When he came of age, he went to the king's palace where he started as a hunter. After one exciting martial exercise, his colleagues accused him of failing to submit a certain animal skin that they had killed two weeks earlier. The king did not take it kindly. On sensing danger, Ndumuhigi decided to seek a soothsayer's advice. The soothsayer told him to simply give the king that animal's skin. So the young man promised the king that he was going to bring the skin.

The following morning, he woke up very early and walked for the whole day. The next day he reached a very large river that was flooded. The skin was on the other side of the river. He put in some magic and the river receded. He crossed and reached a homestead where a monster lived. The same monster collected all the skins that were discarded by hunters in the forest. Since the monster was not in the house, Ndumuhigi entered, took the skin and left. He reached the river and put in some magic and the river receded again. He crossed.

Meanwhile, the monster saw him and ran after him but it found the river so flooded that it could not cross. The monster was so disappointed that it called out Ndumuhigi and told him:

You will find me in the form of cow;
and I will take revenge.
You will find me in the form of a beautiful girl;
and I will take revenge.
You will find me in the form of a sheep;
and I will take revenge.
You will find me in the form of a spear;
and I will take revenge.

Ndumuhigi heard everything that the monster had said but ignored it and continued with his journey. The king was very pleased to receive the skin and gave him many presents. He also allowed him to go back home. Ndumuhigi left the king's palace very happy. On his way home, he saw a sheep following him and he took it with him. After another distance, he spotted a very nice spear and thought as he picked it up:

"This spear befits a man like me."

With his spear, he continued his journey while the sheep ran happily in front of him. Just before he reached home, he saw a very beautiful girl and stopped to greet her. He thought:

"What a beautiful girl! I must propose marriage to her without wasting time. What else am I waiting for in life?"

He proposed marriage to the girl and she agreed. He asked his parents to visit the girl's home to formalize their marriage. Two weeks later, they were declared husband and wife.

As soon as they started living together, Ndumuhigi discovered that his wife was neither a girl nor a boy. This situation greatly frustrated him. However, he decided to keep it to himself because he had pestered his parents to hurry the marriage procedures. Instead, he preferred seeking the soothsayer's advice. But every soothsayer he visited told him that they had never handled such an issue. So Ndumuhigi gave up and decided to live with the problem.

One day, his wife requested him to take her to the forest to look for a particular herbal medicine. Ndumuhigi agreed and the following day, they set off to the forest armed with axes. On reaching a large crocodile-infested river, they stopped. Among big trees that grew on its bank was a thin, branchless eucalyptus whose height superseded all the rest. It was slightly bent such that its top was directly facing the centre of the river. His wife observed it carefully. She noticed that a branch that protruded from the tree top had grown vertically towards the centre of the river. She pointed at it and told her husband:
"There we are, darling! The medicine I want is on that branch."

So the husband climbed the tree and after he had reached the top, the wife grew into a monster. Within a very short time, the monster was joined by several other monsters and without wasting any time, they started chopping down the tree on which Ndumuhigi hung. When the tree was almost falling, a bird in a nearby tree started singing:

Any tree that Ndumuhigi climbs becomes infallible;
nevertheless, it can shake.
Any tree that Ndumuhigi climbs becomes infallible;
nevertheless, it can shake.

On hearing this, the monsters got furious and started chasing the bird. On coming back to the tree, they noticed that it had become firm, without any sign of having been chopped. So the monsters started all over again and when the tree almost fell in the river, the bird came back and resumed its song. The monsters chased it again and when they came back the tree had grown back. This went on again and again. The more the monsters concentrated their effort in cutting down the tree, the more the bird sang its song.

Eventually, Ndumuhigi's mother heard the bird's song. She immediately set her dogs free and directed them towards the river where Ndumuhigi was. The dogs went running, found the monsters and tore them to pieces before eating them. Ndumuhigi climbed down the tree and headed home with the dogs. On the way home, Ndumuhigi found a beehive full of honey. He harvested and ate it all and ignored his dogs. He slapped any dog that tried to approach the honey and made sure that there was nothing left for the dogs to lick. The dogs got angry and decided to eat him. They also made sure that there was no trace of Ndumuhigi anywhere. However, they forgot his heart. It was consumed by the weakest dog which had not been given a chance to share with the stronger dogs. After eating their master, they proceeded home.

On reaching home, Ndumuhigi's mother asked the dogs where they had left their master but they kept quiet. The mother asked them once again and when she noticed that they did not want to answer, she decided to deny them food until they produced Ndumuhigi. So the dogs had a meeting and unanimously decided to bring their master back, lest they died of hunger. Within a short time, Ndumuhigi's body was complete, although he could neither stand nor talk. The dogs tried to figure out what was missing and could not. Then one of the dogs asked its colleagues:
"Who ate Ndumuhigi's heart?"
No dog answered. They asked the smallest dog whether it had eaten their master's heart and it answered in the affirmative, scared of the consequences. The rest of the dogs begged it to bring the heart back and promised to always let it eat before any other dog.

After fixing their master's heart, he woke up immediately and walked towards his mother. The mother was happy and fed the dogs as she had promised. Soon after, Ndumuhigi married another girl and they lived happily afterwards. Ndumuhigi almost perished because of his ignorance and ingratitude.

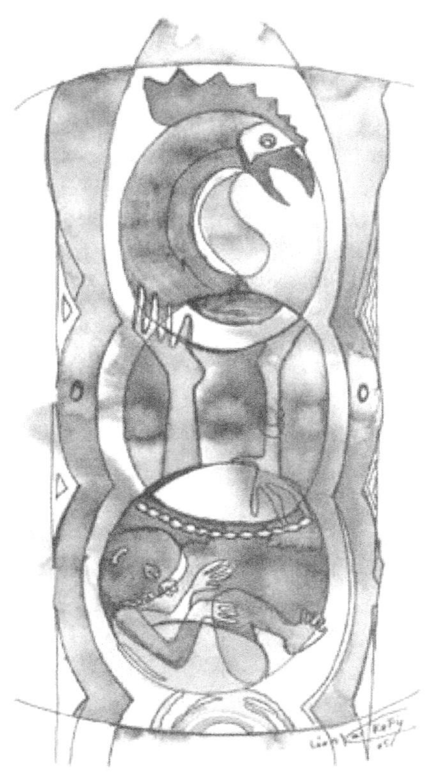

GAKURU, THE TWIN BROTHER

Long ago, there was a man whose wife conceived but failed to give birth. All the other wives who conceived at the same time gave birth several times more, while she remained pregnant.

Other men tried to convince her husband to get rid of her but he remained faithful to his wife. He always told them that he could not chase away his wife without knowing what she was expecting. When his relatives found that he could not abandon his wife, they decided to keep away from him. Even his father snatched back everything he had given him, hoping that his son would one day change his mind but he remained truthful to his wife. Then his relatives plotted to kill him, claiming that the couple was really an embarrassment to their family. At the same time, their country was facing a very hard time. Foreign armies had attacked it from all corners and ruined it. The cattle had been taken away and most wells had been surrounded by thick forests. Their king had been under house arrest for more than twenty years.

One day, the overdue expecting mother was busy preparing food for lunch when she suddenly heard a voice from her womb, saying:

"Mother, please give birth to me now."
"Wait a minute; let me finish preparing lunch for your father. I do not have anyone else to do all this for me. Besides, once I give birth, your father may die of hunger because everyone in this village hates us," answered the shocked mother.

The expected child remained patient and when his mother had finished preparing lunch, he reminded her:
"Okay, now that you have finished doing everything, give birth to me."
The mother went to give birth in her bedroom but the child refused. He instructed her to give birth to him at the fireplace in the cow shed. So the mother went there and gave birth. Traditional midwives tried to separate the child from the umbilical cord but he did not allow them. He did it himself, saying:
"A real man must be able to set himself free!"
He added:
" My brother, who is still in the womb, must be removed quickly but carefully."

His twin brother was born almost immediately. He looked at his brother and marveled. Then he told his mother:
"My twin brother is called Gato, while my name is Gakuru."

Meanwhile, word of the twin brothers' birth spread like bushfire. Those who had planned to kill their father withdrew their plans. Some people were heard saying:
"It is not surprising to hear them talk. They had spent more that fifteen years in their mother's womb"
Others would ask mockingly:
"Are those children bearded? Do they have teeth?"
Such questions prompted sporadic laughter but the comment that greeted the biggest laughter came from one old man who calmly said:
"Those babies must be drunk by now; I saw their father carrying a big pot of wine in the morning."

The following day, the twins asked their father to show them where they could get spears, bows and arrows. After acquiring those weapons, they went to their grandfather and asked why he took away their father's property. On seeing how they were armed, he chose to give them everything he had taken from their father without uttering a word. That day, they led home a very big herd of cattle and their parents were very happy as life returned to normal.

In the evening, they milked the cows and took milk to their mother who was still recuperating in bed. They went to bed early because they had to wake up at the first cock crow to do general cleaning. They also had to clear the overgrown bush around their house. Their father had been too weak to clear it while their mother had remained pregnant all through. Their daily routine, among other activities, included milking the cows, looking after them and taking them to the well to drink.

The twins were actually born at the right time.

Everyone wondered how one-day-old children could do all that. But the children did not pay any attention to what people said. They minded their own business as if they had lived even longer than anyone else in the village.

The twins' courage was witnessed one afternoon when they took the cattle to the well for the first time. Like many wells in the country, that one had been abandoned because of pythons and crocodiles that lived in it and in the nearby swamps. They had killed many herdsmen and their cows. The villagers had tried to kill the animals but failed. Eventually, they decided to abandon the well altogether. When villagers saw the two brothers leading their cattle to that well, they screamed and warned them about the dangerous pythons. The two brothers ignored the villagers' advice and went straight to the well. They cleared the bush around it and all of a sudden, huge pythons appeared from all directions. The two brothers clubbed them one by one until there was none left. They did the same thing to other wells and within one month, all the wells in the country had been redeemed.

Ruyenzi, one of their neighbours, lived on the opposite hill. He had two daughters, Ntonde and Nyirabeza. Both girls had refused to get married. Each would ridicule any man who came to ask their hand in marriage. One day, the two brothers passed near Ruyenzi's house and saw his daughters mocking a young man who had proposed marriage to one of them.

Those girls had prepared a series of very complicated tests that had to be passed by any man who wished to marry them. The two brothers watched how the frustrated young man struggled to pass the tests and felt sorry for him. They also saw that even if he passed the tests, he would end up being mistreated by the girl. So the two brothers went straight to the girls, grabbed them and carried them to their houses. They then informed the girls that they were to stay there as their wives, from then onwards. They went on with their schedules, leaving their wives at home. When they came home in the evening, they found that their wives were busy helping their mother-in-law in her daily work. Everyone was happy. That evening, they enjoyed some wine. The family had grown larger.

News about the strange twin brothers continued spreading and reached their besieged king who noted with appreciation how they had saved the country from the deadly reptiles. He called them secretly to his palace. When they arrived, he asked them to help him liberate the country. They remained at the palace for a few days. They assessed all the possibilities and finally, Gakuru told the king.
"We shall begin from here. We shall first liberate this palace from the enemy, then spread countrywide."
The king thought that it was a good idea and then provided the brothers with any help they needed. In the middle of the night, Gakuru

and his brother attacked the foreign soldiers that had been guarding the palace. By morning, every member of the foreign army had been killed. Gakuru quickly organized the army into two battalions. He asked Gato to lead one of them and within two weeks, the entire country had been liberated. Both armies came home victorious.

When they came back to the palace, they were sorry to find that their king had died on the first day of the battle. He had been shot by a stray arrow and it went unnoticed until the war was over. After mourning their beloved king, the army decided to enthrone Gakuru because, after all, it was he who had organized and led the liberation struggle. Thereafter, Gakuru led his country to great prosperity and developed good relationship with other neighbouring nations.

SEBWUGUGU

A long time ago, there was a man in Rwanda called Sebwugugu. He lived peacefully with his wife in the Central plateau. From there, they could see almost the entire country. On a clear day, they could enjoy the sight of Nyabihu and the Huye hills in the south, the

Nyungwe forest in the west as well as the volcanoes in the North. The Akanyaru and Nyabarongo rivers meandered beautifully on the southern and northern part of the plateau respectively. Food was abundant as the area received plenty of rain. Life was like heaven on earth for the young couple as they were soon blessed with a bouncing baby boy.

Before the child was ten years old, a great famine hit the country. It did not rain for three consecutive years and almost every plant dried up. Only a few aquatic plants grew in what used to be river beds. So, Sebwugugu, his wife and their son decided to leave their village in search of food. They roamed the country until they saw a pumpkin plant that had survived the drought. When they approached it, they were delighted to see plenty of pumpkins. They decided to settle there.

One morning, Sebwugugu asked his wife to bring him a machete. She obliged. He started sharpening it. His wife wondered what her husband wanted to do with the machete,

since there was no bush. Everything else had dried up except the pumpkin plant. Then he told his wife:
"I am going to clear this area of unwanted weed so that this plant may produce healthier pumpkins."
The wife objected, reminding him that every other plant had dried up except that particular one but the husband ignored her advice. He even shouted at her and asked her to shut up. The poor wife could only watch as her husband entered the thicket and accidentally cut the pumpkin's stem, even before he could see any weed. Two days later, the plant had started drying up. Sebwugugu never apologized, though he knew very well that it was due to him that the plant was drying up.

For one month, they survived on the last pumpkins that the plant had produced before it was cut down. Thereafter, they had nothing to eat. One morning, the wife asked her son to escort her and they left their house, never to come back. Towards the evening, she started wondering where they would spend the night. They decided to enter a nearby cave. In the morning, they noticed some grains dropping from a certain hole inside the cave, one grain after the other. The grains included sorghum, maize and millet. Beans and peas could also drop out from the hole at rare intervals. The wife picked them and prepared a meal which she enjoyed together with her son. Life went on well in the cave as food was plenty.

Meanwhile, Sebwugugu was never at peace where he remained. One year had passed without seeing his wife and son. He felt very troubled and lonely. He said to himself:
"I must find my lost wife. I will only settle when I see her, dead or alive."
The following day, he left his house and went looking for his wife. He roamed the wilderness until he saw some smoke and followed where it was coming from. It wasn't long before he noticed that it was coming from a cave. He went towards the cave, entered it and found his wife. His son was busy enjoying

a meal that his mother had just prepared. He observed that they were quite healthy. He looked at his own emaciated body and started sobbing. His wife offered him some food to eat. While he ate, they narrated to each other their experiences.

He was happy to discover the source of the food and promised his wife that he would not disappoint her again. He decided to build huge granaries where he would store the produce. He made one for sorghum, one for millet, and other two for beans and peas respectively. Soon, their granaries were filled. They were happy because they had become the richest couple in the land. Soon, word spread that there was a couple that could feed the whole population and many people came to ask for food from Sebwugugu. He welcomed anybody who visited him and gave them enough food to last several months. He would even encourage visitors to come back for more food whenever there was need to do so. As the drought persisted, an increasing number of people started flocking towards Sebwugugu's rock in search of food.

Then one day, he told his wife:
"This hole is too narrow. See! It can only let out one grain. Since we are receiving so many visitors, I am going to enlarge the hole to satisfy all of them"
The wife objected again but before she could open her mouth to say anything else, her husband was already busy enlarging the hole using his spear. Immediately, the grains stopped dropping. He waited till the following day but nothing came out of the hole. Many months passed before any grain dropped. Soon, all their huge granaries were empty and the couple spent many days without food.

Eventually, the wife left their second home and started roaming the wilderness once again with her son. By that time, the famine had reached its climax as all the swamps in the country had become huge dusty fields.

They wandered the wilderness for the whole day. In the evening, they saw a home on a hilltop and decided to go there to ask for food and accommodation. They found nobody in that home. Instead, they saw many human skulls that were scattered in the compound. She bravely held her son's hand and led him inside the house. She soon discovered that it was a king's palace. The king and other survivors had run away from a very fierce beast that used to harass him, since all his body guards had died of hunger.

That beast occupied the palace after having driven out the king and his entourage. It would wake up very early in the morning to hunt for people as it only fed on human flesh. It would then come back late in the evening. There was plenty of food in that palace. The woman prepared some and ate together with her son. After eating, they climbed to the ceiling and hid themselves there. As soon as it was dark, the beast came carrying a human corpse. The woman watched it from a tiny hole. The beast approached the door. It smelled a strange odor and suspected that there were human beings in the house. It screamed:

"I can smell a human being here. May the human being come and help me put down this corpse that I am carrying?"

The woman heard and saw everything but kept quiet. When the beast had put the corpse down, it pounced on it ferociously and within a few minutes, it pushed the head in the compound, using its paws. It came back inside and fell into a deep sleep. The woman soon noticed that the beast brought home a dead human body to the compound every evening. She had now become used to it. Everyday, she would wait for the beast to go so she could start milking the cows that the king had abandoned. The woman and her son enjoyed basking in the sun during the day, eating and drinking before climbing to the ceiling that had become their bedroom.

One day, while they were sitting under a

shady tree after a heavy meal, Sebwugugu emerged from behind and in a faint voice, whispered:
“How are you, my people?” He looked so pale that it was very difficult for his wife to recognize him. Hunger had done the worst that it could to the poor man. On recognizing her husband, the wife was horrified because she knew that he would betray her and their son, but she could not do anything. Nevertheless, she offered him some food and milk. They again narrated to each other their experience until it was dark. Together, they climbed to the ceiling and soon, the beast came home. It ate the human corpse it had brought and said:
“I can smell a human being. May he come down to chat with me as I am feeling very lonely? I promise that I will reward him handsomely if he gives me company.”
The wife warned her husband but he did not heed her advice. Instead, he told her:
“Look: I will climb down and kill the beast. Then we shall claim this palace, the entire

kingdom and everything that is found within its boundaries."

This time, the wife did not insist because she hoped that the beast would eat him and end her miseries. So, Sebwugugu climbed down and walked towards the beast. He was carrying his spear. The beast was delighted. After the usual introduction, the beast proposed a dance. As they were dancing, the beast thrust its sharp nails in the poor man's ribs. Then the beast shouted:

"Ah! It has been years since I ate a fresh human flesh!"

The beast started by draining the blood before eating Sebwugugu. When it had finished, it threw the head in the compound and then said:

"Wherever there is a man, there must be a woman. Will the woman come down so that we can have a dance?"

When the woman did not come, the beast decided to climb towards the ceiling. The woman together with her son clubbed it several times on the head until it dropped down dead.

The following morning, she woke up very early and beat the royal drum to signal the beast's death. The king heard it and returned to the palace. He declared her a heroine and offered her many rewards. Soon, he proposed to marry her and made her son the kingdom's prime minister. Thereafter, it started raining and the kingdom flourished once again.

BAGABOBARABONA

A long time ago, there was a man called Bagabobarabona who was fondly known to his close friends as Bagabo. Like many Rwandan names, his had a special meaning. His father, who died soon after Bagabo's birth, had decided to name him in reference to the difficult times he had experienced before he got married. When Bagabo became of age, he married and lived happily with his wife on a hilltop, overlooking Byimana. One day, his wife conceived. After several months, she developed an obsessive urge to eat a guinea fowl. So she requested her husband to find her that bird. The husband obliged and the following morning, he set off with his hunting dog. He roamed the whole forest but could not find any guinea fowl. When the sun was almost setting, he decided to set up a trap, after which he went back home, tired and exhausted. The following day, he came to see his trap and found that it had caught a tiny rat. The rat told him:

"Man, please save my life today; I may save yours tomorrow."

Bagabo replied:

"Since you have acknowledged that I am a man, I will save your life."

So he set the rat free. He moved to another site, set up his trap and went back. When he came to check the trap the following morning, he found that a guinea fowl had been caught. He felt very lucky. He happily put it in his bag and went home smiling to himself. His journey was interrupted by a heavy downpour that forced him to seek shelter from a nearby rock. His dog followed him there. Before he could thank God for having created it, a hyena emerged from behind and told him calmly:

"Welcome to my home! Because of this rain, I was worried that I would not find anything to eat today. Now, tell your dog to eat this guinea fowl, and then eat your dog before I eat you." Before the hyena finished saying this, a leopard appeared and said:

"Man, tell your dog to eat the guinea fowl. Then eat your dog. The hyena will eat you before I eat the hyena."

Soon after, a lion appeared and told all those animals:

"I am waiting for all of you to follow the leopard's instructions before I eat it because I am too hungry to keep waiting."

As the lion waited for one animal to eat the other, a rat came to the rock and asked: "What is that noise all about?"
The animals explained to the rat what had happened.
"I see!" said the rat and added:
"Okay. Man, tell your dog to eat the guinea fowl. Then eat your dog. The hyena will eat you before it is eaten by the leopard. The lion must eat the leopard before I eat it."

The bemused lion looked at the tiny rat and tried to scare it off the scene because it thought that such a little creature had no business there. The rat screamed and before long, all the rats in that forest had assembled at the rock. The lion looked left and right and found that the whole place was full of rats with all their teeth out. On seeing this, the lion thought that the rats had come to finish him off. He thought:
"A mighty animal like me should not start a fight with rats. Let me leave the battle for the lesser animals like the leopard and

the hyena."

When the lion left, the leopard got very worried. He thought:

"What if the lion changed its mind and found me here? He would definitely eat me."

So the leopard decided to leave the rock very fast. The hyena thought that the leopard would come back and therefore decided to take off as fast as it could. Soon, Bagabo found himself with only his dog and the bag that contained the guinea fowl. The rat told him:

"Didn't I tell you that I too could save your life? You can now go home peacefully."

Bagabo headed home and gave his wife the guinea fowl. She cooked and ate it happily. But two weeks later, his wife told him that she wanted to eat mushrooms. He told his wife not to worry because plenty of it grew in the nearby valley.

The next morning, he went to the valley and collected a basketful of mushrooms which he carried to his wife. On his way back home, he met people who were looking for a thief who had stolen a cow from the king's herd. They stopped Bagabo and asked him where he was going and what he was carrying. He told them that he had just collected some mushrooms which he was carrying home. When they opened the basket, they found meat. This surprised Bagabo who knew very well that what he was carrying was indeed mushrooms. Then he suggested taking them where he had collected the mushrooms but on reaching there, they found blood and the skeleton of a cow on the very spot where he had collected the mushrooms. This was enough proof that he had stolen the cow.

They took Bagabo to the king's palace. When it was his turn to come and answer his charges, he came acrobatically and hit the king with a heavy kick. He waited for the king to wake up. He pretended to bow down and thrust his hands in the king's eyes before running away as fast as possible. The king's servants followed him.

Bagabo reached a flooded river that he could not cross. When he looked nearby, he noticed some smoke and on careful observation, he saw that the smoke was coming from a hut that belonged to an old woman. He begged her to hide him. His pursuers arrived immediately but when they saw the swollen river, they thought that he had drowned and therefore went back.

After sometime, Bagabo said that he wanted to leave. The old woman escorted him to the river and gave him a magic stick that would help him cross the flooded river. Before she bade him goodbye, she told him to utter the following words to the stick: "Magic stick: perform the magic that you always did for the grandmother!"

On reaching the swollen river, Bagabo wondered whether he should really risk his life by crossing it. He thought for a moment. Then he decided to utter the words to the magic stick. Before he could finish the last words, the stick started hitting him until he started

screaming. Then the magic stick paused and told him:
"I have stopped beating you. Now you can tell me whatever you want. Meanwhile, let me treat the wounds that I have given you before you bleed too much."

Bagabo had been so thoroughly beaten that he could hardly talk. He only murmured:
"Take me across the river."
Immediately, he found himself on the other side of the river. Then the magic stick said:
"This is your chance to tell me everything you wish in your life."
Bagabo thought for a while and then replied:
"I want many herds of cattle and a large number of servants to look after them."
To his amazement, he saw more herds of cattle than he had imagined. Then, his wife appeared from nowhere and joined him. They were reunited and lived happily thereafter.

Is there anything in a name?

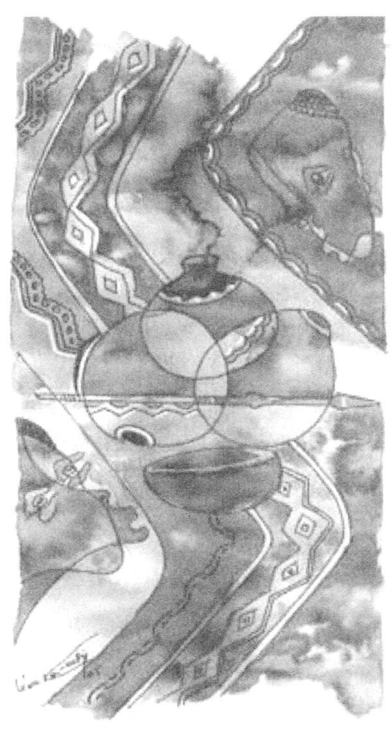

THE TOP SECRET

A long time ago, there was a couple who lived on the shores of Lake Muhazi. That part of Rwanda was abundant with all sorts of crops. Large herds of very healthy cattle decorated the gentle hills around the beautiful lake,

which meandered Buganza Region. Life was heaven on earth for the young couple.
However, their happiness was short-lived as the husband was unfaithful to his wife. Long before he got married, he had developed an insatiable urge for any woman he could lay his hands on. Soon, everybody including his wife knew of his indecent behaviour and tried to dissuade him from it but he could not heed their advice. He frequently beat his wife thoroughly whenever she asked about it.

One day as he was roaming the hills in pursuit of women, he met a hyena. The hyena told him:
"You have just committed adultery with your friend's wife, eh?"
Before the man could answer, the hyena went on:
"Now you must repeat the same act with me, right here and now, or I will eat you."
The poor man obliged and when the hyena was satisfied, she told the man:
"In case I become pregnant, you must take

care of my baby."
The man accepted without hesitating, after which the hyena allowed him to go.

He was so frightened that he stayed indoors for several months. His wife and everyone in the village thought that he had changed his behaviour. Even when he finally decided to venture out, he chose to avoid the trail in where he met the hyena. But the hyena knew all the possible paths the man could use. So when she was about to give birth, she looked for him and told him:
"I am expecting your baby and I will give birth next month. You must bring me some presents."
After one month, the hyena waylaid her man and told him:
"I gave birth to a baby girl. You must come and see her with many presents."

One fine morning, the man carried many presents and went to see his daughter. He marveled when he noticed that the baby was

a very cute girl that was his own replica. He offered the presents to her mother amid terse instructions that scared him, such as:
"My child must neither be caned nor slapped. Nobody should even attempt to throw a stone at my child. I will promptly eat you all, the moment I hear that my child is either scorned or mistreated in any way." The man agreed.

Two years later, the hyena looked for the man again and this time, she told him:
"Your daughter is big enough. You must take her with you now."
So the man took his daughter and presented her to his real wife. The wife did not bother to ask whose child it was because she knew her husband's behaviour. In any case, he would not have told her the truth. However, the man clearly explained to his wife how the child should be treated, to which the wife agreed. The girl resembled any ordinary human being and in fact, her beauty surpassed by far, any other girl in the village. By the time she was about twelve, she could look after her

father's cows. One evening, her step-mother noticed that one cow was missing. The step-mother asked what had happened to the cow. The girl kept quiet. When her step-mother reported the incident to her husband, he simply told her that he already had too many cows and that she should not worry when only one of them could not be traced, though he knew his daughter had actually eaten the animal.

One day, when the step-mother was out of the house, he advised his daughter to behave like human beings by taking good care of cows. The girl agreed. They both promised each other to keep top secret the fact that her mother was a hyena.

From then onwards, she followed her parents' advice and acquired dancing skills and other valuable social graces. She attracted considerable admiration from many young men. Her melodious voice was unequaled and people marveled whenever she danced. By the time she was eighteen, even her parents had become famous in that region because of their daughter's meticulous approach to whatever she did. She became exemplary and an idol to all her colleagues.

It did not come as a surprise when many young men competed for her hand in marriage. She finally accepted the land's most handsome and well-behaved young man as her future husband. In those days, after the dowry had been paid, it was customary for the bridegroom to collect his bride from his father-in-law's homestead. He would be accompanied by his own father as well as other close relatives and friends. In return, the bride's parents and friends would accompany the girl to her new home. That was the equivalent of today's wedding day.

It was a sunny morning when the bridegroom came to collect his bride. Both parties were well prepared for the event, such that very little time was spent at the bride's homestead. The bride's father accompanied her daughter amidst songs and dances. Then he shouted:

"My daughter, remember to keep the secret!" Some people stared at him but soon forgot what he had said and continued singing. After a few hours, he shouted again:
"My daughter, remember to keep the secret!" This time, some people started mumbling, not knowing what to say. The bride's father remained on one side of the hill and let the procession cross a valley to climb the hill just opposite him, singing all along. Once the procession had reached a parallel level, he repeated the message at the top of his voice:
"My daughter, remember to keep the secret!" This brought the music to an abrupt halt. The procession stopped, wondering what was wrong with the man. When they saw him walking back to his village, they resumed singing and continued their journey.

Although few people paid any attention to the bride's father, the secret worried the bridegroom's father more than anything else. After the festivities, he called his daughter-in-law and sought to know what the secret was, to which she said that she would find time to tell him. Weeks, months and years passed as he kept asking his daughter-in-law what the top secret was. One day, she told her father-in-law that she would reveal the secret after giving birth to her third child. The old man was patient and when he saw her giving birth to her third child, he was so happy that he offered her a cow.

The old man waited patiently as he calculated the time. He knew that he would finally know the secret. Then one day, he went to his daughter-in-law and found her talking to the child. She knew exactly what he wanted. After offering him some wine, she told him: "The day after tomorrow, in the evening, please come so that I may tell you the secret. I know that you have been patient for a very long time."

The old man was so excited that he could sleep for neither night. Meanwhile, the daughter in law prepared some wine. On the promised day, she served the wine in the early afternoon such that her husband and his friends would get drunk by the time the old man arrived.

It was a delicious wine. Her husband's friends kept reminding him how lucky he was for marrying such a wife. The husband marveled on hearing such praises, for he knew that she was even more beautiful than they thought she was. Soon, the old man came. His daughter-in-law ushered him into a separate room, saying that the young men could disturb him. He was offered some wine. On the first sip, the old man confessed that it was the best wine he had ever tasted ever since he started drinking alcohol. His daughter-in-law smiled gently, which made the wine more delicious. He felt very lucky and privileged.

Then she closed the door to the room and all of a sudden, stripped herself naked and became a hyena. Immediately, flames started burning from both her mouth and bottom. The fire-spitting hyena started growling at the poor old man who, in return, screamed for help. Nobody heard his screams because everyone was drunk and asleep. The hyena exhaled one powerful flame that threw the old man down. Using her strong claws, she picked him up and made him sit upright. She gave him a long stare as if to remind him that he asked for it. She then turned the other way and exhaled an even stronger flame from her bottom that blew the old man to the wall and kept him breathless for some minutes.

She dressed, regained her human form and joined her husband, who was already asleep. Her husband had drunk so much wine that evening that he did not know what happened to his father. However, he managed to wake up early to say good morning to his father. He could not believe his eyes when he saw the old man stretched on the floor, dead.

A top secret should remain secret.

THE LION MAN

Once upon a time, there lived a man and his wife on a hill. They had two children: a boy and a girl. They lived happily and enjoyed a good relationship that existed between them and their neighbours. One day, the man's wife died. He continued taking good care of his two children. But he soon got bored of staying single and approached a certain lady who told him that she could only accept him if he killed his two children. Every woman that the man approached told him the same thing, until he gave up. He decided to stay with his children.

The children were barely teenagers when a great famine hit the country. It did not rain for a very long time. All the crops and the pasture dried up. Many people and animals died of hunger. It is said that no woman or animal gave birth throughout the famine. So the village elders decided to seek advice from soothsayers and find out what they should do to stop the famine. They told them that the cause of that famine was the existence of the two children whose mother had died. They also said that in order to reverse that situation, the two children had to be isolated in another country. That advice motivated the father, because no woman would accept him. Furthermore, he thought, the whole country was suffering because of his children. So, he decided to send them away in isolation.

One evening, he asked his daughter to prepare enough food to carry as they had to take a very long journey the following day, to a country where there was plenty of food. The daughter did as her father said and they set off very early the following morning. They walked until they reached a very thick forest. They entered it and when they reached in the middle, where the father knew very well that the children could not find their way back home, he dodged them and came back home, leaving his own children alone in that forest.

It was not long before the children noticed that their father had vanished. They tried calling him but he did not answer. When they realized that they had been left alone, they decided to go even further on their own. They walked and walked until they became very exhausted. They reached a pool of water. The boy was tempted to drink from the pool but his sister warned him against such an act, as he would become a lion. This is how they had been taught by their parents. But the boy was soon overwhelmed by thirst and decided to drink the water. He became a lion immediately. However, the lion told his sister not to worry as he would protect her instead of eating her. Besides, the lion told her that they would continue talking and staying together as usual.

They roamed the forest until they saw a huge tree whose branches had many delicious fruits. They decided to climb it and enjoy those fruits. Soon, the tree became their home. The lion would go hunting while the sister remained in the tree preparing food. Life went on like that until hunters noticed the tree. They had been attracted by its delicious fruits. As they picked fruits, they were surprised to find a very beautiful girl in the same tree. They went back and reported the news to the king.

The following morning, the king went to the site to verify what he had been told. On reaching there, he saw the girl and was amazed by her beauty. He ordered the hunters to ask the girl to climb down. The girl refused. Instead, she sought help from her lion brother. He did not hear her because he was very far away. Meanwhile, the hunters threatened to cut down the tree. The girl was scared and therefore agreed to climb down. Immediately, they carried her to the king's palace. Nevertheless, she kept screaming along the way and somehow, her lion brother heard her cries.

The lion followed his sister to the king's palace. When the king's army tried to kill it, the sister objected and they left it alone to enter the palace. It was not long before they realized that the lion was harmless, after all. When the king noticed that the lion behaved like a human being, he ordered his subjects to construct a separate house for it. He even instructed them to look for a young woman to stay with the lion and care for it. The lion would become a human being during the night and turn into a lion during the day.

The lion and the young woman lived happily as husband and wife and after one year, the woman gave birth. By the time she had her third baby, most people in the palace had realized that the lion was indeed a disguised human being and they tried to find ways to rectify the situation. So the woman's friends advised her to keep her children out in the rain and prevent them from entering the house unless their father opened the door for them. One day, when it was raining heavily, she did as her friends advised. The children begged to enter but instead of opening, the mother told them to ask their father to do so. As the father could not bear his children's cries, he jumped out of the lion's skin and went to open the door for his children.

Meanwhile, his wife took the lion's skin and threw it into a big fire that she had prepared.

As it was burning down, herds of cattle, sheep and many herdsmen came out of the flame. Soon, the whole compound was full of sheep and cattle. This was a happy surprise for the king who was forced to give the lion man a bigger space that could accommodate all the cattle and sheep.

Another famine hit their country and forced many people to wander from place to place in search of food. It is in this circumstance that his father reached the lion man's homestead and begged for food. The lion man recognized him but his father did not. He gave him a warm welcome but did not reveal himself to his father. He told his servants to give the man enough to eat and then prepare for him a warm place to sleep. The following day, he introduced himself as his father's real son and then narrated how he survived after he abandoned him and his sister in the forest. The father was extremely embarrassed and in the evening, when nobody was watching him, he committed suicide.

When the son learnt about this the following day, he was very sad. He could only mourn his father's death as there was nothing else he could do.

NGUNDA

Long ago, there lived an extraordinary man in Northern Rwanda called Ngunda. In just one sitting, this man could eat so much food that even twenty men could not finish. But the more he ate, the more he worked. It took a whole month for his area's population to plant where he had cultivated for only one day. It is said that all the hills in Rwanda are actually mounds that Ngunda prepared to grow potatoes. Because he consumed a lot of food, one wife alone could not satisfy his feeding habits. So he married six very hard-working wives who would prepare enough food for him.

With the help of all the villagers, the six wives would prepare as much food as possible and deliver it to her husband's hut before dusk one day of the week. This was because it was not possible for them to prepare a meal on a daily basis. When his wives had brought all the food to his hut, he would eat all of it and then wait for a whole week before he had another meal. This did not stop him from working. He could work for several days without eating or drinking anything. The fact that he could eat so much food had greatly frustrated his fellow villagers as they spent so much time preparing his food.

Ngunda was generous too. One day, he decided to visit one of his in-laws and help them till their land. On reaching there, he asked them to provide him with fifty hoes for him to use in digging. They gave them to him. Within one hour, he had finished both sides of one hill and before midday, five hills were ready for planting. He could even have doubled the cultivated area but he had broken all the hoes into very small pieces. Meanwhile his father-in-law invited all his neighbours to help him plant. They could not finish because the cultivated area was too big for them. It took them many weeks to plant all of it.

That evening, Ngunda's father-in-law slaughtered a fat bull, kept the leg for the family's consumption and gave the rest of the meat to their son-in-law. They also gave him umutsima, which is a paste made of sorghum or millet. Other accompaniments included banana and sorghum wines in great quantities such that the entire hut had no more space left except for Ngunda alone. He cleared the entire meat and drank all the wine.

When he was brought some water to wash his hands, he said:
"I have tasted the meat; whoever ate it must have really enjoyed it!"
The servant who had brought him the water went back very surprised and reported to Ngunda's in-laws who were equally astonished.
"Our son in law is still hungry. Please, prepare for him whatever is available so that he may, at least, feel that he has eaten something worthwhile," said Ngunda's father-in-law.
So they prepared the only meat that had remained and gave it to Ngunda. They also gathered all the wine from the nearby villages and gave it to him. Ngunda ate and drank everything but never got satisfied. He went to his home vowing never to make any other visit to that particular father-in-law.

As he became more and more aware of his embarrassing greed, news of his insatiable nature spread quickly countrywide. One day, he sat by himself and wondered whether he was really a normal human being. He considered all the food he had to eat, all the wine he had to drink, all the labour and the number of people involved in preparing that food and felt awful.

"But look! I am the only man on earth who can cultivate such a large area. Who else can? The more I eat, the more I work. I am therefore not as greedy as people claim. In fact, I am a hero!"

That day, the king had hired people to till his land and, as it was a custom, he had prepared plenty of food and banana wine to satisfy every worker.

"Eh… by the way, why didn't the king invite me? Let me go there and find out," said Ngunda to himself.

When he reached the king's palace, he told the king:

"Long live the King! Will his Majesty the

King allow me to say why I have come here?"
"Permission granted," said the king.
"Your Majesty, I have come here to greet you and to ask for food. I also heard that you invited all the strong men from this village to cultivate for you. I do not know why I was left out. All of those you have invited put together can not even cultivate a half of my day's work. Why was I left out?"
"This was not an oversight, Ngunda. I was worried about how I would feed you."
"Your Majesty. Let me just have a mouthful of wine and then go back to my house. I do not want to embarrass you today," said Ngunda.
"Okay," said the king. "Go and see the person in charge of beverages but do not do anything silly."

Ngunda had a drinking straw that he always carried with him wherever he went. He told the man in charge of drinks that the king had authorized him to have just a sip of the wine. Because the man was very busy, he showed

Ngunda one large pot and continued with his work. Ngunda drank all the wine that was stored in that room and tiptoed out quietly before the man could notice anything. He walked back home wondering whether the king was really serious by preparing such a small quantity of wine for all those workers he had seen.

"I alone have drunk it within five minutes and am still thirsty. The king should not blame me. The wine was too little and besides, he knows my drinking capacity."

He continued his journey feeling sorry about the king. On reaching home, he found that one of his wives had given birth. He straight away proceeded to his in-laws to ask for presents. On reaching there, he told his father-in-law:

"Your daughter has given birth. Send her some presents."

Before the father-in-law could utter any word, Ngunda pointed at two very huge granaries full of sorghum in the compound.

"In fact, those two can do," he said, as he approached the granaries in a hurry.
He put one on his shoulder and the other one on his chest and immediately went home as his in-laws watched in amazement. He started chewing the raw sorghum as soon as he left the gate and before long, the first granary was empty. He threw it away and started on the second and finished it also. But he felt so thirsty that he found it difficult to take another step. He sat for a while and glanced at a valley below. He saw a herdsman preparing a well for his cows. Ngunda asked him:

"Hey, Brother! "Would you please let me drink some water from your well? I am dying of thirst."
The shepherd obliged. Ngunda bent his huge body over the well and after several sips, the well was dry. He sat near it and soon fell asleep, without even thanking the shepherd.

As the thirsty and frustrated cows grazed near the well, two bulls started fighting. Suddenly, the fattest one accidentally stepped on Ngunda's stomach and burst it, killing him instantly. The terrified herdsman quickly rounded up his herd and led it home where he announced the good news. Everyone in the village felt relieved. Even his wives did not bemoan his death.

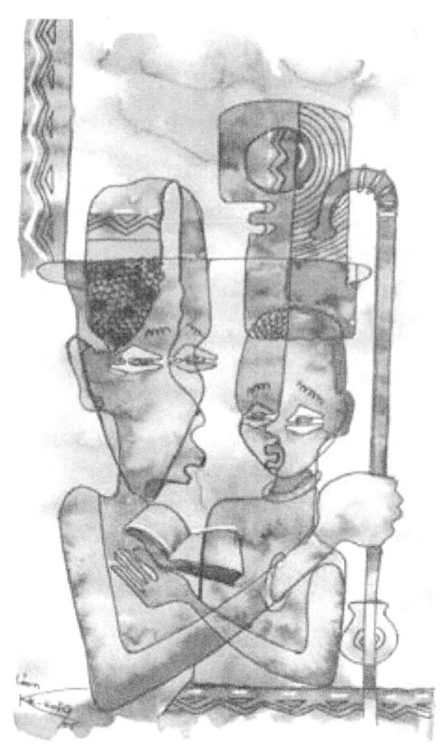

NTAMWETE AND NDABIKUNZE

A long time ago, there were two brothers who lived on the Eastern shores of Lake Kivu. The elder one was called Ntamwete, while his brother's name was Ndabikunze. They had inherited a lot of wealth from their father. Their land stretched from the lake and extended to Gishwati, where they kept cattle. Ntamwete was lazy and liked spending most of his time drinking wine. He quickly became an alcoholic and could not manage his family. After having sold all his property to pay his debts, his wife left him and found another husband. Ntamwete did not care and concentrated on his wine-drinking sprees. Soon, he could no longer afford any drink and started begging.

For Ndabikunze, life was totally different as the young man was hard working and much disciplined. He did not have time for drinking wine because he was always busy supervising his farm workers and looking after his cattle. The more he worked, the more his wealth increased. News about his prosperity spread all over the region.

Ntamwete grew envious about his brother's success. He started plotting ways to kill him so that he could inherit his vast wealth. An idea came to his mind: He called some of his friends and asked them to prepare for him

a big coffin. Once the coffin was ready, he called his younger brother and told him:
"I am getting worn out because of old age. I have ordered a coffin in which I wish to be buried once I die. I would like you to check for me whether the carpenters made it to my specifications."
His younger brother agreed. The following day, they went to inspect the coffin. On reaching the carpenter's workshop, he asked his brother to lie in it. This, he said, would help him assess the coffin. His younger brother hoped into the coffin and lay down, the same way a dead body is laid. Immediately, a group of four very strong men emerged from within the workshop and covered the coffin. It was Ntamwete who had organized the gang. They had planned to put his younger brother in that coffin and throw him into the lake, alive. Then, Ntamwete would come and inherit his brother's wealth of which he would give a considerable share to the gang.

As Ndabikunze struggled to get out of the

coffin, the men carrying it run very fast. He could feel them going down hill and knew that they were going towards the lake. They continued hurriedly but they soon got tired and thirsty. They decided to put down the coffin in order to find something to drink. They left it along the footpath and did not worry because they had used very long nails to fasten it. They saw a woman who was digging. They begged her to tell them where they could buy some banana wine. The woman who saw them carrying a coffin was sympathetic. She thought that they were going to bury their dead relative. She invited them to her house on the other side of the hill. She offered them her condolences and recounted how she felt when her second child died just one month earlier. The feelings were still fresh in her mind. She cried softly as she offered them wine.

Meanwhile, a herdsman passed near the coffin and wondered what was inside. He had never seen a coffin before. He decided to

shake it. Ndabikunze asked from inside the coffin:
"Who is opening this coffin?"
The herdsman was surprised to note that there was someone in the coffin. He asked why he was in that box, to which Ndabikunze replied:
"My people wanted to make me their king, but I refused. So they got very disappointed with me and decided to throw me into the lake. If you are interested in becoming their king, come into this box and tell them that you have accepted their proposal. They will be very pleased to hear that. They will then take you back to their land and enthrone you instantly."
On hearing this, the herdsman forgot about his cattle and opened the coffin. Ndabikunze replaced the cover using the same long nails and took the cows with him. It was a large herd of healthy cattle.

Meanwhile, Ntamwete's group kept enjoying the banana wine, oblivious to what was

going on with the box. Eventually, they staggered back to where they had left it. On hearing them, the impatient herdsman shouted from inside the coffin:
"Take me back to my land. I have now accepted to be your king. Do you hear me?"
They ignored him and continued towards the lake where they duly threw him in. They felt satisfied after their wicked act. They walked back arguing how they would divide Ndabikunze's wealth among themselves. Finally, they agreed on who would take what and continued with their journey more contented than ever.

On reaching home, the first person they saw was Ndabikunze. They could not believe their eyes. They approached him and stared at him, dumbfounded. They asked him:
"Are you not the Ndabikunze we threw into the lake?
Ndabikunze replied that he was indeed the one.
"Then what happened? Where and how did

you get such a large herd of cattle?" they demanded nervously.

Ndabikunze cleared his throat and told them:

"Listen, Brothers: When you took me to the lake, I thought that you were my enemies but I was wrong because you took me to the source of all the cows on earth. I managed to bring only these ones because I was alone. In actual fact, I would like to request you to kindly take me back there so that I may bring an additional herd."

They asked him to describe the exact place and Ndabikunze mentioned the place where they threw the herdsman.

They looked at one another.

"Uhm! We need to prepare more coffins and get our own cattle from the lake. This time, it is Ndabikunze who will take us and throw us in there."

So they went back to the workshop and asked the carpenter to prepare a large coffin in which all of them could fit. After one week, the coffin was ready. They decided to carry their own coffin all the way to the lake and have it covered there. That way, they thought that it would be easier for Ndabikunze to push it into the lake.

They smiled broadly all the way to the lake. When they reached it, they hired more people to help Ndabikunze push the coffin into the water. There was no time to waste. The gang hurriedly entered the coffin. With the help of the hired men, Ndabikunze, covered it and watched it sink into the deep lake. He remained motionless for a while. Suddenly, he sprinted towards Gishwati without saying a word to the hired men who had helped him push the coffin. The men looked in disbelief as Ndabikunze climbed the hill as fast as his legs could carry him. Then, they became conscious of what they had done. They felt extremely sorry but there was nobody to apologize to. They stayed there, silent and confused. Then, their legs started trembling as if they were too weak to carry their bodies.

They soon collapsed, stretched their limbs as if they were swimming in turbulent water until they all became motionless. Within a short time, their bodies had become as dark as charcoal. To this day, nobody can stand there and stay alive for more than ten minutes.

GATWAZA

There was once a man who lived with his wife on Ngoma hill, in Southern Rwanda. He owned a big track of land on which he used one section to grow various types of crops while the rest was allocated for cattle.

Since the man was an only child from his parents, his community despised him because he did not have relatives. This situation was worsened by the fact that the couple had one girl child. It was very unfortunate for the couple because, in those days, a family which would not provide a warrior to defend his nation in times of war was considered useless.

When the man realized that his wife could not give birth to other children, he decided to provide his only daughter with a boy's training. Her name was also changed to Gatwaza and was trained in various martial tactics where she excelled. She grew up into such a fierce warrior that her prowess spread throughout the region. In archery, she had never missed her target and she could accurately hit an object one kilometre away. In wrestling, no man had ever beaten her while her high jump record remained unbeaten for many centuries. Above all, nobody knew that she was a girl except two neighbours.

Neighbours soon grew envious of Gatwaza's father. They tried to kill him so that they would inherit his wealth but they failed. Then they decided to report him to the king. They told him that there was a man in Ngoma who despised His Majesty, adding that he even collaborated with foreign armies in order to overthrow the kingdom. They also informed the king that this man did not have a son to help defend the nation in case of invasion. The king summoned the man immediately. On reaching the royal palace, the king told him:

"Man, I have been informed that you are very rich while you do not have anyone to inherit your vast wealth. I therefore want to split your property and divide it among those who can contribute to the country's security in case of foreign invasion. You may then join your collaborators and stay in their country."

The man informed the king that all those were lies, adding that he actually had a son whose name was Gatwaza. On hearing this, the king knew that his accusers were liars because he had heard of that name and all the praise associated with it. He exclaimed: “So you are the proud father of the famous Gatwaza? I would like you to send him here as soon as possible. Since he is your only child, I will give you several faithful servants who will also protect you against your enemies.”

Gatwaza’s colleagues had never known she was a girl. They had always seen her in boy’s attire. She had not developed breasts because of her strenuous exercises. Besides, her father had explained to her their state of affairs which motivated her to try her very best to look like a boy. She had done this to her own and her father’s satisfaction.

One week later, Gatwaza appeared at the royal palace, accompanied by her father. They were welcomed and Gatwaza was introduced. Soon, interviews which were aimed at determining her skills in archery, long and high jump as well as wrestling were administered. The king was amazed at Gatwaza’s capabilities and wondered why nobody had informed him about it. He was convinced beyond doubt that Gatwaza was the country's most skilled young man. He therefore selected ten servants and asked them to accompany Gatwaza's father back to his home. He asked them to protect him and stay with him. He then bade them goodbye.

The following day, Gatwaza accompanied the king on a hunting exercise. In those days, hunting was a very useful exercise that idle warriors turned to in times of peace. They would carefully plan an ambush for the unsuspecting animal in exactly the same way they would do for their enemy before any attack. The best target was the animal's neck. Once hit, the animal would be rendered motionless due to its broken neck. An arrow that hit the animal's limbs would be considered amiss while warriors who were responsible for such misses would be excluded from the king's group in future hunting exercises.

A herd of buffaloes was sighted grazing, about one hundred metres from where the king was. The hunters cautiously observed the herd for some time after which they chose their target. They took their positions. They crawled stealthily until they reached twenty metres from the unwary herd. Using a secret code that served as an order to attack, a swarm of arrows whistled towards the targeted animal. It lay down instantly while the rest of the beasts scampered for dear life. The hunters walked towards the fallen buffalo. There was only one arrow that had hit the neck. It was Gatwaza's. The king marveled and went home convinced that with a sharpshooter like Gatwaza, his kingdom was invincible.

After some time, the king planned an invasion against a neighbouring kingdom that had threatened him several months earlier. That kingdom's army had occupied part of his territory for a long time. Plans were made and one day before they left for the war front, the queen requested her husband to leave behind Gatwaza to protect her. The king agreed and the following day, they left. In the evening, the queen asked Gatwaza to stay in the palace. After everyone else had gone to sleep, she called Gatwaza, offered him some good wine, and then told him:

"You see how I have painfully tried to convince the king to leave you behind. It is because I love you. I want you to spend with me all the nights that the king will be away on the war front. Nobody will ever know about it."

Gatwaza objected and replied to the queen:

"It is well known that if Her Majesty indulges in such acts, the king never comes back from the war front."

The queen tried to convince Gatwaza that nothing would happen to the king but Gatwaza ignored her. In her futile attempt to persuade Gatwaza, she said:

"If the king died, I would make sure that you inherit the kingdom. In such circumstances, you would be the king while I would be your wife and the queen."

This disturbed Gatwaza who left her alone and chose to remain at the gate throughout the king's absence.

The worried queen decided to take revenge. When the king came back from the war front, she accused Gatwaza of having tried to sleep with her. This greatly upset the king who called Gatwaza immediately. He asked people to tie him up to be beheaded. After being tied, he asked for permission to say his last word, but in the absence of everyone else. The king obliged and asked everybody to leave. Then Gatwaza stripped naked. The king was surprised to notice that Gatwaza was indeed a girl. Due to lack of exercises, her breasts had been well developed. It is at this point that he realized what his wife had tried to do. Gatwaza had always looked like a very handsome boy who had secretly attracted the queen and other female servants within the royal palace.

The king called his wife who was dumb

founded by what she saw. She decided to run away from the royal palace. Servants tried to stop her but the king intervened. He asked them to let her go wherever she wanted. He asked Gatwaza to dress up. Then he called his advisors and narrated to them the whole episode. They unanimously advised him to take Gatwaza as his wife. Thereafter, they had many children and their kingdom flourished.

MUNYANA

A long time ago, there was a man whose wife gave birth to boys only. The boys grew up, built their own homes and married hard-working wives who bore them healthy children. In those days, almost all house chores were the wives' responsibility while their husbands spent most of their time drinking wine whenever they were not at the king's palace. Being married to brothers from one family, it was naturally convenient for the wives to carry out their errands together. Thus, they would collect hay together except when one of them was sick. Even then, they would look after her and provide her with food until she recovered. Working together provided them with an excellent opportunity to gossip about their common mother-in-law and life in general. They discussed practically anything: from how their husbands behaved when they had drunk too much wine, to how their children looked alike.

Sometimes, while gathering hay, each wife would narrate her unpleasant experiences with their mother-in-law. One wife would relate how, on many occasions, her mother-in-law had asked her whether she really suited her son. Another wife would be heard saying: "I will call that woman to witness how

her drunken son snores the whole night." This would make them laugh and probably make their day. It was during one of such serious gossips that a voice from the womb of one expecting wife was heard, saying:
"I must discover the bone of contention between a mother and her daughter- in-law."
They were taken aback. Each woman quickly picked up her load of hay and ran to her house, without a word. They did not meet for several weeks and whenever they did, they preferred talking about other issues.

Life continued as usual. More children were born while those who were mature enough got married and bore other children. The mother whose child spoke from the womb gave birth to a beautiful baby girl. They called her Munyana. After several days, the mother realized that the baby was mute. Though she could not speak, she proved to be more intelligent, compared to other children of her age. When she was mature enough, she got married in the neighbouring village.

Munyana's marriage coincided with her husband's sister's marriage. Soon both women were expecting and gave birth at the same time and this trend continued until they could not give birth anymore. Munyana gave birth to boys only while her sister-in-law only had baby girls. Whenever they gave birth, the mother-in-law would exchange the babies such that Munyana ended up with all the girls while her baby boys were given to her sister-in-law. Because she was mute, nobody else knew what was taking place except her mother and sister-in-law. Nevertheless, she accepted the baby girls but kept a close watch on the other children, for they lived in the same village.

One day, her sister-in-law told her:
"I am going to find sticks for my boys."
Munyana, to the amazement of her sister-in-law, replied in very clear language:
"Let me also get some for my associates."
Those words scared Munyana's sister-in-law. She rushed to seek advice from her mother-

in-law who could not believe it, saying:
"Remember how many times I exchanged the babies and tell me whether a normal person can tolerate it. If it were you, wouldn't you have objected?" adding that Munyana's silence over such issues proved beyond any reasonable doubt that she was deaf.

One evening, as they finished eating supper, Munyana surprised her husband when she said:
"Would you do me a favor, darling?"
Her husband went outside to find the person who had asked for a favor and when he could not find anybody, he came back to the house, even more confused. Then his wife asked him:
"Do you have to find me the answer from outside?"
The husband, still confused, told her that he had not expected her to talk, since he had never heard her do so. He promised to do anything she would ask him. Then his wife told him: "Prepare a very good wine and when it

is ready, invite all our relatives. I will then tell them something that has been disturbing me. In the meantime, please do not talk to me because I want to start talking on that day."

One week later, the invited relatives assembled at Munyana's home. They drank, ate and danced to traditional music. It was a happy day. Then Munyana's husband stood up, told the guests the purpose of the get-together and signaled his wife. Everybody in the gathering knew that Munyana could not speak. They wondered what a mute person was going to tell them, and furthermore, how she was going to do it. Munyana cleared her throat and started by thanking the astonished guests for having accepted her husband's invitation.

The crowd gazed at her in disbelief, as she went on:

"I got married in the same week my sister-in-law got married to my husband's brother. We always conceived and gave birth at the same time till we were unable to conceive any more. I always gave birth to boys. My mother-in-law would give my baby boy to my sister-in-law each time I gave birth. As a result, all my children are these very boys that you always call my sister-in-law's sons. These children that are known as my daughters belong to my sister-in-law."

People started murmuring as the father-in-law's face showed a mixture of shock and embarrassment. All the guests were disappointed. They looked for the mother-in-law and the daughter-in-law so that they could answer those accusations. They asked them to stand up but their legs failed them because of fear and shame. The father in law stood up, cleared his voice and said:
"My daughter, you took good care of my granddaughters as your sister-in-law did to my grandsons. All the children are well. Take your sons and still remain the mother to my granddaughters. Meanwhile, your mother-in-law together with her daughter should leave this homestead for good."

Both women left immediately without uttering any word or even looking back. It was total silence as the guests, including the shocked and helpless banished wife's husband watched them leave in humiliation. Stressed faces and tearful eyes followed the two creatures as they trailed the meandering footpath that led them to an unknown world. Soon, guests started disappearing, one by one. Meanwhile, Munyana went on chatting with her excited children, her father-in-law and her delighted husband. She was happy. A new phase of life had started.

THE ABANDONED GIRL

Once upon a time, there was a beautiful girl in a small village. She had lost her mother when she was still young. Her father married another wife who mistreated the child. Her step-mother always gave her a lot of work.

Her father was aware that his wife mistreated the child but he could not do anything about it for fear of causing commotion within the house.
"When an opportunity comes," he thought, "I will offer my daughter to whoever would wish to marry her so that I will have peace with my wife."

One day, a man came to ask for the daughter's hand in marriage and the father quickly agreed. The formal custom procedures were observed and within a very short time, a colourful wedding ceremony took place. After the wedding, when all the guests had gone home and the new wife was sleeping, a voice came from above and said:
"Girl, this man is not your husband. Yours is yet to come. Wake up and go back to your parents now."
She quickly awoke and went back to her parents. She told her father everything she had heard. He accepted her and asked her to feel free and have patience. Two months later,

another man came to ask for her hand in marriage and the same process was repeated. After the wedding, when all the guests had gone home, she received the same instructions from the same voice and she went back to her parents. One more marriage took place thereafter but the same thing happened. News of her failed marriages spread quickly in the region. This embarrassed her father.

In those days, every adult male was obliged to render some services at the king's palace. The girl's third marriage coincided with her father's turn to report to the king's palace. Her ther was therefore scheduled to leave the next day. Before the father left, he asked his daughter to leave the homestead and start fending for herself. He told her that he was so embarrassed by her failed marriages that he did not wish to see her anymore. The father asked one of his servants to take her to a forest, very far away and abandon her there. He made sure his daughter left the homestead before he started his own journey to the king's palace.

Her trek was very long and tiresome. They reached the forest at sunset. They entered it and when they reached the middle, the servant abandoned the girl and went back to the village. She was so exhausted that she could not walk any more. She sat under one of the huge trees and fell fast asleep. She started wandering in the forest the following morning and before midday, she noticed something that looked like a house. She cautiously walked towards it and found that it was a nice house that had been deserted. In the compound, there were two granaries full of beans and sorghum.

She entered and swept it. She went picking wild fruits and came back to the house where she hid herself in one of the rooms. She slowly started feeling free. On the second day, she lit a fire, prepared herself a hearty meal and lay on the bed. She started wondering about the person who built the house.
"Why did he choose to build it in this forest? From where did he harvest these beans and

sorghum? Why did he abandon his harvest?" The most probable answer, to her own thinking, was that the house had been built by a thief who one day was eaten by a wild animal.

"Did the animal find him lying on this bed?" That thought made her jump out of the bed. She chose to sit outside and watch the animal coming instead of being eaten from that bed.

It was a cold afternoon as it had rained continuously for several days. There was a flat stone in the compound that served as a bench. Though it was still wet, she decided to sit on it and continued imagining things. Then, she heard some cracks nearby. She got scared. She looked in the direction of the noise. She noticed something moving. A closer observation revealed that it was a tired and equally afraid man. He looked as if he had not seen food for days. He looked at the girl and said: "Greetings! My name is Mwungeri. I am on a long journey to the king's palace and I need accommodation for tonight. Would you let me stay here?"

The girl welcomed him and told him that she was feeling lonely and very happy to find someone she could talk to. She lit a big fire that made her visitor feel warm. She prepared food and something to drink. They ate, drank and chatted. During their conversation, she told him how she ended up being in the house. On his part, the man told her that he had not eaten anything for four days besides being rained on day and night. They both felt comfortable with each other and found that they actually shared the same problems, a fact that naturally created an urge for them to stay together. She found no need to prepare a separate bed for her visitor. They had become one. They continued talking until they finally fell asleep.

At the first cock crow, she heard the same voice again, but this time, it said: "You have finally found a husband and a home. You must not break any of the marriage vows and you must obey the king."

She woke up. She remembered the handsome young men who had paid a lot of dowry to her father, including the cattle and beautiful fields her former spouses owned. Then she wondered how she would spend her entire life in the middle of that forest, with an old man as her husband. While she was still asking herself all those questions, the forest cleared and became a very beautiful pasture with many herds of healthy cattle. Her house became a palace, with busy servants running around.

Mwungeri was awoken by the servants' activities. He was confused. He thought he was dreaming when the young woman told him:
"What you are seeing is real and has come from God. However, God has commanded us to remain faithful to one another and to obey the king."
Mwungeri agreed as he continued marveling at God's kindness. He finally said: "I came here yesterday seeking accommodation in a dangerous forest. Now I am

surrounded by servants, all this wealth and, above all, you as my wife! We must surely obey God at all cost," he concluded. He felt the happiest man in the world.

Soon, it was his turn to serve at the king's palace. Months and years passed. Mwungeri's services had become indispensable there. His wife kept waiting but soon grew impatient. She turned to her servants whom she enticed with very good presents. She would prepare for them excellent wines. Once they were drunk, she would invite to her bed whomever she chose among them. That trend continued for as long as her husband remained away. Meanwhile, Mwungeri had become one of the king's top advisors. Back home, his wife had been contented with her servants.

One morning, she could not believe herself when she woke up and found herself in a pool of water full of noisy frogs and other aquatic creatures. The beautiful pasture had become a large swamp. News of the incident reached

Mwungeri. He asked for leave and found his wife roaming about near the swamp, not knowing what to do. Mwungeri knew that she had disobeyed God's instructions. He asked her what had happened. He first apologized for having stayed for so long without visiting her. On her part, she truthfully told her husband everything she had done during his absence. They forgave each other and immediately, God gave them another pasture, filled it with cattle and gave them new servants. When the king heard about it, he was very sorry and decided never to hold his subjects at the palace for too long.

More than a dozen Rwandan stories in one book

Book: From the Heart of Africa

Author: Timothy Njoroge

Language: English

Volume: 144 pages

Reviewed by: Martin Bishop

Available at: Most local book libraries

IF the aim of writing From the Heart of Africa was to revive cultural virtues like resilience, courage, respect, patience and others in young people, then he is half way there. This 144 paged book is rich with more than a dozen Rwandan stories. Although it was meant for young people, adults too can find a lot of hidden wisdom in this small treasure.

The book is inspirational! It drips with life lessons from which anyone can learn. Among the various stories, the book features Ngunda, a powerful and hardworking giant! It is said that all the hills in Rwanda are actually mounds that Ngunda prepared to grow potatoes. Or a story of families pushed to the edge by famine and how they fought for survival.

The book also tells of the tale of a hunter who can hear animals speak to each other, a story of a man who outwits his jealous brother who is scheming to kill him and many other well-known folktales passed down from generation to generation.

Writing this book, Njoroge kept all levels of readers in mind, as it's an easy read written in plain English. Every story in this book has a moral. The evil are punished and the good live happily ever after.

These stories may be myths filled with funny animals and giants and they may seem to have taken place hundreds of years ago, but they are relatable for today's readers because they deal with global situations.

Source: **https://www.newtimes.co.rw/section/read/104881**

Printed in Great Britain
by Amazon

33412928R00086